PLANTING & BUILDING

RAISING A JEWISH CHILD

NEW, COMPLETELY REVISED EDITION

PLANTING & BUILDING

RAISING A JEWISH CHILD

RABBI SHLOMO WOLBE

TRANSLATED BY RABBI LEIB KELEMEN
EDITED BY A TALMID

FELDHEIM PUBLISHERS
JERUSALEM • NEW YORK

First published 1999
Newly revised edition 2000
ISBN 1-58330-402-9

FELDHEIM PUBLISHERS
POB 35002 / Jerusalem, Israel
200 Airport Executive Park
Nanuet, NY 10954
www.feldheim.com
Printed in Israel

Library of Congress Cataloging-in-Publication Data

Volbeh, Shelomoh.
[Zeri'ah u-vinyan be-hinukh. English]
Planting & building : raising a Jewish child / Shlomo Wolbe ; translated by Leib Kelemen ; edited by a talmid.
p. cm.
Includes bibliographical references.
ISBN 1-58330-402-9
1. Jewish religious education of children. I. Title: Planting and building. II. Title.
BM103 .V6513 2000
296.6'8'083--dc21 00-023842

In loving memory of my dear father

לזכרון עולם

סעדיה אליעזר בן יהושע ניסן זאקארין

I did not have the privilege of benefiting from his presence beyond my early childhood. Nevertheless, my beloved father succeeded in imbuing me with both pride in Yiddishkeit and love for Torah.

Many will read this sefer and improve their skills in raising Yiddishe kinder in the ways of Torah. May this zechus stand to his credit. And may the publication of this sefer, which is dedicated to my father, increase the merit to our family, so that we may raise our children to middos tovos, ahavas Yisrael, and ahavas Torah.

יחזקאל חיים וחנה הינדא זאקארין

I was happy to see this fine translation of זריעה ובניין בחינוך *and wish to express my gratitude to Rabbi Leib Kelemen and Rabbi Z.E.G. for their dedicated efforts to bring this work to the English-speaking public.*

S. Wolbe

Contents

Preface

We joyously present the English-speaking reader with a translation of the sefer, זריעה ובניין בחינוך, by Rav Shlomo Wolbe, *shlita.* I personally wish to thank my revered Rebbi for affording me the opportunity to assist in the presentation of this work.

Please note the following background information, so that you may derive maximum benefit from this sefer.

1. This book, in its English translation, is the product of many hours of work by an exceptionally talented individual, Rabbi Leib Kelemen. A successful author in his own right, he selflessly applied himself to this work for almost two years. The original Hebrew edition was prepared by Rabbi Yosef ben Shachar from a series of tape-recorded lectures given by Rav Wolbe to a group of Bnei Torah at the Beis Ha-mussar in Yerushalayim. This book is a translation of that sefer. Although Rav Wolbe, *shlita*, reviewed the Hebrew edition extensively, this English translation was entrusted to my inadequate hands. Please recognize that any flaws contained herein are solely a product of my own inadequacy, rather than any defect in the original source of the information.

2. Since this work was originally presented in the form of a lecture series, the material was never meant to be an all-encompassing, detailed handbook on chinuch. Rather it is a general guide for intelligent individuals who will use the guidelines presented here as a catalyst to inspire the betterment of their own chinuch skills. As Chazal say, תן לחכם ויחכם עוד.

3. Rav Wolbe, *shlita*, is always very concise in his presentation, and therefore I advise the reader to read and reread every part of this book many times in order to achieve the full benefit of the author's intent.

So now, dear reader, open your heart to the wisdom of the leading *mechanech* in our generation, and prepare yourself for the great challenge of chinuch, which begins with ourselves. May Hashem help us all in this formidable task, so that we may bring our children to their fulfillment – bringing *nachas ruach* to *Ha-kadosh Baruch Hu*, and thereby, nachas to us.

ויהי נועם ה׳ אלוקינו עלינו ומעשה ידינו כוננה עלינו
ומעשה ידינו כוננהו

Z.E.G.
Yerushalayim

Introduction

Chinuch (education) is a mission of the highest priority, a mission whose success guarantees the continuity of the Jewish People and its Torah. Chinuch is also a responsibility assigned to every father and mother, and one cannot excuse oneself from it, saying "This isn't my job." Furthermore, chinuch is a task that parents naturally long to perform; from deep within themselves, parents yearn to educate their children properly.

Even though education is a natural yearning and responsibility, it is also a deep wisdom. It cannot be mastered after a bit of casual consideration or by depending on one's hunches. Parents and teachers cannot rely on their God-given intuition alone and assume that is enough and everything will turn out all right.

Today few people realize that chinuch of children is an art that requires study and attentiveness. Unfortunately, often even teachers working in the field lack this awareness. In order to educate children properly, we must understand what education really means. We must organize and define all the different components of our standard educational methods, identifying which actions are really educational, which have nothing to do with chinuch, and which are the antithesis of chinuch and even produce undesirable results.

Sometimes we use methods that are counterproductive because we assume that they contribute to the educational process, but further investigation — especially keeping the long-term in mind — actually reveals that these techniques hinder education. We must carefully examine and define all the components in this third category of educational methods, understand why people might mistakenly think such actions work, and then see why they really are anti-educational.

Today, there is a severe lack of awareness that chinuch is a wisdom which requires study. Sometimes this awareness doesn't exist even among teachers. If we are to educate properly, we must act out of deep thought, proper definitions, and attentiveness. Finally, even after careful study of all the components of education, we hope and pray that Hashem will be satisfied with our efforts and grant us success.

I Growth and Construction

DUAL PROCESSES IN DIVINE GUIDANCE

Two complementary processes lie beneath all progress and development in the world, and the better we understand them, the better we will be at encouraging and shaping the development of our children and students.

We see references to these complementary processes in the Shemoneh Esrei (the Eighteen Benedictions or Amidah prayer). There we find two blessings that relate to the *geulah* (final Redemption): "Blessed are You, Hashem, Who builds Yerushalayim" and "Blessed are You, Hashem, Who causes salvation to sprout." The first blessing refers to the *construction* of Yerushalayim, and the second refers to *growth* towards *Mashiach* (the Messiah).

Growth is a natural, organic process. Seeds placed into the soil will sprout on their own. So will trees and flowers. In contrast, *construction* is a *manual process*. A person lays the building's foundation, and then places brick upon brick until he finally completes the structure.

The Creator of the universe uses these same two processes to direct the world towards its ultimate perfection. On one hand, Hashem builds, intervening in human history. On the other hand, Hashem causes the coming of Mashiach to grow naturally. Thus, redemption is always described in organic terms: The second blessing of the Shemoneh Esrei describes the King Who "makes deliverance *sprout forth.*" The Mashiach will blossom forth from the stalk of his ancestor, Yishai. The prophet Zechariah (3:8) actually calls the Mashiach by the name *Tzemach* — *"Sprout."*

THE SAME TWO PROCESSES PRODUCE PERSONAL DEVELOPMENT

The very same processes that Hashem uses to perfect the world we can also use to perfect the human being. Rabbi Moshe Chayim Luzzatto (Ramchal) begins his book *Mesillas Yesharim* with the words, "The foundation of Chassidus (piety) and the root of perfect service of Hashem is understanding and appreciating one's obligation in one's personal world." It is tempting to gloss over the apparently repetitive phraseology, "The foundation of Chassidus" and "the root of perfect service of Hashem," or to assume that Ramchal contrived this parallel structure just to ensure that the first letters of the Hebrew words would spell out the four-letter name of Hashem. This cavalier approach to *Mesillas Yesharim*, however, obviates any hope of understanding his meaning. In this short phrase, Ramchal teaches us that there are two, parallel processes in serving Hashem.

The first one, Chassidus, demands a *foundation*. Chassidus constitutes the top floor in the *construction of a human being*, and *construction* always requires a *foundation*. The taller and loftier the building we wish to construct, the deeper the foundation we must dig. To reach the heights of Chassidus, we must first lay a strong foundation and then build on it.

The second one, Divine service, evolves organically from within, and such growth requires a *root*, Ramchal hints. Where there is no root, there can be no growth. In one terse sentence, Ramchal informs us that we must be involved in both construction (building ourselves through the acquisition of *ma'alos* — good qualities) and growth (sowing internal seeds that will sprout during our lifetime). And with this understanding we should learn the remainder of the introduction to the *Mesillas Yesharim*.

THE JEWISH CALENDAR REFLECTS THESE TWO PROCESSES

These dual processes of human development are echoed in the two Days of Awe, Rosh Hashanah and Yom Kippur.

Although Rosh Hashanah launches the Ten Days of Repentance, which lead up to Yom Kippur, we do not confess any sins on that day. The first day of the year is dedicated entirely to renewal of Divine sovereignty in the world and accepting Hashem's authority over ourselves. With this beginning, we *plant* the seeds of our inner life for the coming year. This is what our Sages mean when they tell us that, "A year that begins in *poverty*" — with a sense of how limited we are compared to Hashem — "ends *prosperously*." Our Divine service sprouts forth each year from the powerful impression left by Rosh Hashanah.

On Yom Kippur, on the other hand, we actively confess our sins and search for ways to perfect our character; the day climaxes in the Ne'ilah service, when we make concrete commitments to reconstruct ourselves.

PLANTING AND BUILDING IN CHINUCH

In this same way we should understand the idea of sprouting and construction in childhood education (and in the process of educating ourselves!). If we want the child to grow into a Jew who learns Torah and fulfills mitzvos, we must *plant* in him the seeds of Torah. This is what Chazal (the Sages of the Talmud) meant when they said:

> When a child knows how to speak, his father should teach him Torah and the Shema. Which Torah? Rabbi Hamnunah specified [to teach him the verse], "Moshe commanded the Torah to us."[1] (*Sukkah* 42b)

---

1 *Devarim* 33:4.

These words will be the root of the child's speech.

This is planting. The child first hears that we have a Torah, and that we had a great prophet, Moshe Rabbenu, and he commanded us to accept the Torah and its mitzvos. Of course, after the grain is planted and begins to sprout, it needs rain. So too with a child. After the first planting, he needs "rain" that will saturate him and make him sprout. With a child, this is the warm environment of the home and the warm relationship he has with his father and mother; and together with this, the living example of parents who perform mitzvos happily and say blessings with intention.

About *construction* in chinuch, we find the following in *Pirkei Avos* (5:21): "At five years of age, the child should learn Tanach; at ten, Mishnah; and at fifteen, Gemara." Here Chazal teach us that there are levels in the process of building a man into a *talmid chacham* (Torah scholar), and the chinuch at each of these levels must match the child's natural development. This is a great chinuch principle: It is forbidden to demand of a child things that, because of his limited maturity, he is not yet capable of understanding or doing. He will be disgusted by these things and will try to escape them to whatever extent he can; and this damages his spiritual development.

A child is a living creature. He grows, and as his body grows so too his soul grows — he grows spiritually. A child's growth needs attentive care, like the growth of a tree or grain. Special emphasis needs to be placed on organic processes. If we want something particular to sprout, we must be careful to plant precisely what we want, and afterward the seeds will sprout from themselves in a natural process.

On the other hand, there is construction. We must build a mensch. It is impossible to depend on sprouting alone.

If I build the child and help him acquire *ma'alos*, but I don't relate to his *koach ha-tzemichah* (innate growth potential), then his *koach ha-tzemichah* will slowly wither and the child will be a robot. He will probably do what he is told, but he won't possess any internal vitality. When this child matures he will continue to do what he must, but he won't possess individual initiative, since initiative flows from *koach ha-tzemichah*, and the *koach ha-tzemichah* long ago withered away and rotted. All that is left is a human robot.

If we allow a child to sprout and grow without building him, the result is a wild man. If we build a child without relating to his *koach ha-tzemichah*, we turn him into a robot. Chinuch consists of both the *koach ha-tzemichah* and the action of building. That is, we must build a child while cultivating his spiritual potentials.

THE IMPORTANCE OF TIMING

We mentioned the *mishnah*, "At five years of age, the child should learn Tanach; at ten, Mishnah; and at fifteen, Gemara." Why not earlier? Why not teach a child Tanach at age three? Here Chazal established that a child's growth proceeds in stages. A certain period arrives when a child is ripe to learn Tanach, and then we teach him Tanach. Together with this the child grows further. When the child reaches the age of ten, his growth has proceeded to the point where he is capable of learning Mishnah. After five more years he matures more, and he reaches the age of Talmud study.

As we have seen, Chazal here established that a child has stages, and the stages proceed according to the child's organic *tzemichah* — according to the child's natural way of growth. During childhood the child passes from period to period. We must recognize these periods *and relate to them at the appropriate time.*

From these words of Chazal we see the seriousness of chinuch, and the seriousness of precisely timing our chinuch efforts to match the child's stages of development.

THE RIGHT TIME — THE STARTING POINT

It is written in *Parashas Ekev*, "And you shall teach them to your children, to speak of them." Here Chazal comment (*Sukkah* 42a):

> When a child knows how to speak his father should teach him Torah and the Shema. Which Torah? Rav Hamnunah said, "*Torah tzivah lanu Moshe.*"

> In the *Sifri* (*Devarim* 46) we find:

> From here they said that when an infant begins to speak his father should speak with him in *Lashon ha-Kodesh* (the Holy Tongue, i.e. Hebrew) and teach him Torah; and if he doesn't speak

> with him in *Lashon ha-Kodesh* and teach him Torah, it is as if he buried him, as the verse says, "And you shall teach them to your children, to speak of them." If you teach them to your children — "you and your children will have long days" — but if you do not — then you will have short days.

Chazal express themselves powerfully and affirm that if we don't precisely grab the moment that the child begins to speak and immediately begin to speak with him in *Lashon ha-Kodesh*, "*Torah tzivah lanu Moshe*," it is as if we buried him. Why is the moment so serious? The beginning of speech is the right time for planting *emunah* (belief), and when we begin to speak with him in *Lashon ha-Kodesh* — this is the planting itself. If the planting is done when the ground is prepared — the planting will be successful, and the sprouting begins. If we delay the season — the land is no longer ready.

This is very similar to what we see in the agricultural world. There are specific times for planting: At the beginning of the winter we plant, and if we delay until the rains come it is already impossible to plant. If we put down seed too late, the seed rots in the ground and nothing will sprout from it.

Also if we act too early we won't be successful, for the land is not yet fertile. We must grab the right moment. "When the child *begins to speak* — his father should speak with him in *Lashon ha-Kodesh* and teach him Torah."

These are the foundations of the "Beginning Point," the moment of planting, the beginning of the serial stages of chinuch. Rashi in *Parashas Lech Lecha* comments, on the verse (*Bereshis* 14:14), "*Vayarak es chanichav*": "Chinuch means the *beginning* of a person's or tool's entry into its future profession. This is also the meaning of ***chanoch*** *la-na'ar*, ***chanukas*** *ha-Mizbe'ach*, and ***chanukas*** *ha-Bayis*."

The concept of chinuch according to Rashi is the appropriate entry and the beginning point. This is *chanoch la-na'ar*. When a child reaches a certain state we need to plant in him what he is ready to absorb at that time.

If we don't teach him the appropriate thing at the appropriate time, it is as if we buried him. If one doesn't grab the fertile moment, the right plant will not sprout. From this sort of planting, there will not sprout a man who *lives* with *emunah* or with Torah. Therefore, it is as if we *buried* him.

Throughout the Torah the beginning point is especially significant. Whether we are dealing with the beginning of the year (Rosh Hashanah), or the beginning of the week, or the beginning of the month (*Rosh Chodesh*), all beginnings have special significance. The beginning is the period when we can plant something. Seeds planted after the season won't take root.

This presents a clear demand on parents: They must recognize more or less the period the child is passing through during his maturation, and they must *match their demands to his ability in every period.* If they ask more than the child can do — i.e. when the child is not yet sufficiently mature to understand what his parents want from him — this is terribly damaging educationally. This sort of seeding cannot take root. The child cannot develop via something he cannot understand. The child must proceed in stages and pass gradually through the various periods of childhood.

In this presentation we are not trying to define these periods. That belongs in a separate talk. Rather, we are focusing on the essentials of chinuch according to the Torah.

We will now offer several common examples of inconsistency between the child's ability and the requests made of him.

Something very common: Mothers pride themselves on toilet-training their children at an early age. The earlier they "succeed" at training the child, the more pride they feel. It is accepted today, and I concur with this opinion, that if we force a child out of diapers too early this damages the child's development. The time will come when the child himself will want to be trained, and then the process will proceed far more harmoniously.

Another example: Often we don't relate sufficiently to the child's play. For the child, play is a serious matter. Rabbi Yisrael Salanter used to say: When a child plays with a piece of wood in the bath, and he pretends that it is a ship, if we take the piece of wood away from him he has the same experience an adult would have if a real ship of his sunk. For the child, the piece of wood is like an adult's ship. When an adult interferes in a child's play, he steals something from the child.

Certain errors are widespread and are accepted as norms. For example: People demand that their children sit at the Shabbos table throughout the meal, even though the meal can extend for an hour, ninety minutes, or sometimes even longer. A young child can't sit quietly so long. He needs to frolic. If we force him to sit through the entire meal, we are compelling him to do something far beyond his ability, and we need not explain how destructive this is. The intention is good: We want to build. But for the sake of building, we push the child beyond his ability; and children can't be built with demands that are beyond them. Ultimately, such demands damage the child. The damage is especially serious when the demands are made of young children, since even the smallest interference at the time of planting can produce serious aftereffects.

A LONG-TERM PERSPECTIVE

Chinuch is a process which demands a long-term perspective. When a child is two or three years old, we must know and take into account that when he turns fourteen or fifteen he will be in a difficult stage. In order to pass through the fourteen-year-old stage peacefully, the child needs to have a warm bond with his parents. If parents are rough with their two-, three- or four-year old — if they discipline him harshly, hit him, and make demands beyond his ability — they destroy the warm relationship. Indeed, at such an early stage the problem in the relationship won't be obvious. The child still needs his parents; he loves his parents. But later, when the child is fourteen, the surprised parents come to me crying and exclaim, "I don't understand what's happened to my child. He doesn't speak with me at all. He tells me nothing. I have no idea what's going on with him." When the parents come and ask me what to do, I ask them: "Tell me, did you strike the child when he was three?" The father answers, "Of course, I had to educate him." Then I respond: "Now you are paying for the blows you gave him back then." The spankings and rough treatment ferment in the child's subconscience without even the child's awareness. The memories are hidden within his soul. But in adolescence the effects surface, and the parents see that they have destroyed their relationship with their child. For the parents this is terribly painful, and for the child it is terribly damaging.

Early childhood education must have a long-term perspective. Parents must build such a warm relationship with their child that the relationship will survive and assist the child even during the difficult period of adolescence.

Sometimes it appears that we get better results with harsh approaches. However, "*Ha-chacham einav b'rosho* — The wise man looks ahead!" Parents who know the secret of chinuch and the importance of a long-term perspective are very careful in the early years not just to focus on immediate results. It's very common that the child won't listen to me, and I give him a few slaps, and instantly he listens. I proudly think, "Ah, I know how to influence my child." However, this is a very premature celebration. Parents will pay for such reactions when the child reaches age fourteen or fifteen, and then it will be very difficult to repair the damage.

CUSTOMIZED EDUCATION

Parents need to recognize their child's unique character. No two children are alike. If parents don't know this, and therefore they assume a child possesses potentials that he doesn't, the chinuch and efforts they invest in their child won't match the child.

"Educate a child according to *his way*; even when he grows old he will not depart from it" (*Mishlei* 22:6). If I want to educate a child, I must contemplate and examine what this particular child's way is.

It is obvious that a banana plant needs different care than an apple tree. If I raise a banana plant and an apple tree, and provide both of them with identical care, at least one of them won't grow well, and perhaps neither will! The same is true of children. I must discover the child's traits and take them into account.

On the verse in *Mishlei* mentioned above the Vilna Gaon comments:

> Educate a child according to his way — when he is still a child — and then when he grows old he will not depart from it. The idea here is that a person cannot break his way, that is, the *mazal* (the astrological sign which determines a person's character) he was born into…

The Vilna Gaon explains that certain things can't be changed. Citing the Gemara (*Shabbos* 156a), "He who is born under the astrological sign of *Tzeddek* (Libra) will be righteous…,"[2] the Gaon then continues:

> Rather, free will is given to man to utilize his *mazal* as he wishes. He can choose to be a *tzaddik* (righteous person), *rasha* (wicked person), or *beinoni* (average person), as the Gemara (ibid.) says: He who is born under the astrological sign of *Ma'adim* (Aries) will be a blood spiller. Rav Ashi explained: He may be a bloodletter, a thief, a *shochet* (ritual slaughterer), or a *mohel* (ritual circumciser).

The Gaon goes on to explain that each of Rav Ashi's illustrations are telling. If the fellow is a *tzaddik*, he will use his blood-spilling inclination to be a *mohel*—for a mitzvah. If he is a *beinoni*, he will be a *shochet*. This is also a blood-spilling profession. It isn't a mitzvah like *milah*; however, if someone wants to eat meat, he needs a *shochet*. So, too, the bloodletter. If, however, he is a *rasha*, God forbid, then he will use his *Ma'adim* potential for murder.

Someone born under the astrological sign of *Ma'adim* may use this potential for any one of the professions discussed above or anything similar to them, depending on his moral stature. However, one cannot change someone fundamentally, transforming him from the sort of person born under the astrological sign of

---

[2] The above gemara has nothing to do with present-day astrology.

Ma'adim into the sort of person born under the astrological sign of *Tzeddek*.

For example: A child whose nature is to be constantly active cannot be transformed into someone who sits and reads twenty hours a day. If we force the child to do so, we will damage or lose him. Later, the child will go his own way and do whatever likes, which might be different from what his parents intended.

The Gaon continues:

> The idea is that [King] David is described as a reddish fellow, which is why [the prophet] Shemuel erred upon seeing his face...

Shemuel was terrified by David ha-Melech (King David). He saw that David was "reddish, possessed of beautiful eyes" (*Shemuel* I 16:12). "Reddish" — He was born under the astrological sign of *Ma'adim*. But still he was "possessed of beautiful eyes" — He would only spill blood with the permission of the Sanhedrin.[3]

The Gaon concludes:

> This is the meaning of the verse, "Educate a child according to his way" — according to his *mazal* and nature you should educate him to do mitzvos — then "even when he grows old he will not depart from it." However, if you force him against his *mazal*, now he will listen because he fears you; but later, when the time arrives for lifting your yoke from his neck, he will turn from

[3] See Midrash *Yalkut Shimoni, Shemuel* 124.

what you have taught him, since it is impossible to break one's *mazal.*

If you force him into a different track, one inappropriate for his nature, he will indeed listen to you now, and you won't notice that any damage has been done. However, later, when he matures and no longer fears you, he will no longer listen to you. This is a fundamental educational principle.

There are parents who err in this, and this error has catastrophic consequences. I remember when a famous *tzaddik* brought his son to the yeshiva. When he presented his son, he told us that the boy was shy. Indeed, the boy didn't speak. When we asked him questions, he failed to respond. However, we later discovered that the boy's silence wasn't a product of shyness. The father, because of his great "righteousness," didn't allow his children to leave the house or play — since "they must learn!" Games are "a waste of time!" The boy was consumed with hatred for his father. I didn't succeed in removing this hatred from the boy's heart. When he grew up, he entirely rejected the Yoke of Heaven and married a secular woman; and all this flowed from very well-intentioned chinuch — to make him into a *tzaddik.* The father didn't take into account the boy's personality. As we said, this sort of chinuch produces catastrophic results.

THE GENERAL PRINCIPLE

From all that we have said, we can understand a bit about what chinuch is. Chinuch must allow the child to sprout, according to his way, and accordingly we build further his behavior and *middos* (character traits). If we don't allow him to sprout, as we said, the child will be a robot. However, if we depend on sprouting alone, and we don't build his *middos* at the right time, a wild plant will sprout — a wild man.

II Fundamental Chinuch Principles

PERSONAL EXAMPLE

Parents' greatest responsibility is to serve as an example. Every child naturally wants to identify with his parents and imitate them. If their personal example is good, and if the relationship between the parents and the child is healthy, a warm and heartfelt relationship, then a boy will naturally want to be like his father and a girl will naturally want to be like her mother. One of the most important essentials of chinuch is personal example. If parents demand of their children things that they themselves aren't doing, they risk corrupting the children entirely.

EXPLANATION

In the growth process of the child there must be explanation — explanation of *emunah* and of the Torah's mitzvos. Parents are obligated to explain to their children. They should not think that the child is too young and therefore must fulfill things without explanation. Explanation must be provided appropriate to the child's level of development. But we must not avoid explanations. To our distress, this job is often ignored. We aren't involved enough in explanation.

LOVE

Let us contemplate a bit the paths of chinuch. When we want to educate our children, which paths must we walk?

One of the great biologists discovered something amazing. He compared the state of different animals at birth to the state of a child on his day of birth. It became clear that the child, as far as his structure and development went, needed another year of gestation in order to reach the state of animals at birth. That is, nine months of gestation is precisely half of what a child needs to complete his initial development.

As is well-known, any animal is far more independent at birth than a human infant. When a kitten is born, he already jumps. The same is true of horses and all other animals. On the day of birth they are already active. When a child is born, however, he is like a block of wood. He can't do anything. Only after a year will the child develop the abilities all animals possess when they are born. The biologist argued that this is no accident. The first year of growth constitutes the second half of gestation, and its purpose is to provide a "social womb" which encompasses the family. During "the second half of gestation" the child must forge relationships with his father, mother, brothers and sisters, since this is the mission and purpose of man, to live in community — unlike animals who live for themselves.

The conclusion we draw from this is that the infant must live in the family "crib." In other words: warmth. Once, kibbutz children were raised in children's homes. There they were cared for. When the children were young, mothers came during the day to nurse them and care for them, but the children slept in the children's homes. Over time, the kibbutzim changed the approach, and today infants sleep in the parents' home. Why did this change come? Because they saw that the children's development was impaired. A child needs the warmth of a home, and the definition of warmth is love. A lot of love. A child grows only when he is loved.

PUNISHMENT

Here we touch upon a topic that everyone asks about: punishing children. There is a prevalent opinion that the essence of chinuch is accomplished with punishment. To my distress, this opinion is also prevalent among teachers. One school principal published a wonderful book on chinuch, but he called the book *When To Punish the Child*. I asked him why he had to give that name to his book, given that the book touches on many other topics. Why does our perspective have to be: "When should we punish?" Punishment should be the last card in chinuch. Our perspective should not be "When should we punish?"

Punishment expresses parents' desire to control. A person feels that if he can punish, he has control. The same is true of a rebbe in his classroom. Once a man presented himself to us as a candidate for *mashgiach* (spiritual supervisor) of the *yeshivah ketanah* (yeshiva secondary school). One of the questions he asked me was about the sort of authority he would possess: Would he have the authority to expel a child from the yeshiva? This was his first question. I saw that he would never develop into a *mashgiach* or *mechanech* (educator). If this is his initial perspective — "When is it okay to expel a child?" — if the authority to expel is what gives him the feeling that he is in charge — then he can't function as a *mashgiach* or *mechanech* in a yeshiva. This is an invalid approach.

The same is true of parents. If their whole perspective is "When to punish?" — this is a perverse approach that undercuts the basis of any sort of healthy chinuch.

But isn't it true that "He who withholds the rod hates his son,"[4] and that one must beat one's child?

In another verse we find, "So I herded the flock of slaughter, indeed the poorest of the flock; and I took for myself two rods; the one I called pleasantness, and the other I called damaging; and I fed the flock" (*Zechariah* 11:7). Here we see that there is a rod with which we "damage" and hit, and there is another rod that we also

---

[4] *Mishlei* 13:24.

use to educate, but with pleasantness: the "rod of pleasantness."[5]

One must know that the rod of pleasantness is also a rod, but it doesn't necessarily cause pain. If I give a child encouragement, this is also a rod. If the child does something good and I give him a piece of chocolate, this is also a rod; but it is a rod of pleasantness.

It is impossible to estimate how much damage someone does to a child when he gives him a serious spanking. Rabbi Eliyahu Lopian *zt"l* would always say to us: "With children — only in a pleasant way." He said that when he got older he regretted every spanking he gave to his children when they were small. Rabbi Eliyahu raised eleven children, and many of them became great *roshei yeshivah*.

Chazal say (*Bereshis Rabbah* 10) that each and every blade of grass has a *mazal* that beats it and tells it to grow. That is, the force that causes growth Chazal call a "blow" — the "blow" that says grow! Of course, the intention is not that an angel with white wings and pink cheeks armed with a baton sits on every blade of grass and hits it. Chazal's intention is to say that there is a force that causes grass to grow, and that force, in the language of Chazal, is called a "blow."

This is how we should understand the "rod" mentioned in the verse, "He who withholds the rod hates his son." There is no need to understand this verse only

---

[5] See *Sanhedrin* 24a.

in a sense of hitting the child. There are other ways to guide his growth, better ways.

In this regard, I want to add something I still see. In the Gemara (*Kiddushin* 30) there is a discussion about when it is no longer permitted to spank a child: age sixteen or age twenty-four. According to either opinion, if a father strikes his son beyond the age limit, he violates the prohibition of "*Lifnei Iver* (misguiding the uninformed)," since his son will rebel and might hit back. The reality today is that if we spank a three year old, we violate the prohibition of "*Lifnei Iver*." We see that the child rebels against his father. You can see that a child who receives a slap wants to slap back. He lifts his hand, but he can't reach his father's face. There is only movement, but the movement is clear. The child rebels. This rebellion must be taken into account. In previous generations the situation was different. Children had more tolerance, and therefore they could tolerate spankings. Children also had stronger character. It didn't damage them to receive a few blows. However, today the whole environment is one of rebellion, especially here in Eretz Yisrael. If someone tries to crush a child by spanking him, he can hurt the child and his relationship with the child, and when the child grows up he might close himself off from his parents. Then it will be impossible to build a trusting relationship, an open relationship.

Indeed, it is true that there are unusual situations of pressure. For example, in a home where there are a number of children, all of whom need to go to sleep and are screaming, if the mother is exhausted from the day she might slap the children to achieve quiet. I am not speaking of a rare event like this. This is an unplanned response to an emergency — "first aid" — and won't happen every week or even every month. I am warning against intentionally incorporating slapping and spanking into one's approach. This is destructive.

Screaming at a child is as bad as, or perhaps worse than, spanking a child. If you pay attention, you see that when a father screams at his son, the child is so terrified that he begins to tremble. The scream so severely affects the child's nerves that be begins to shake. Screaming is worse than a light slap. True, it is difficult to control oneself: When the father arrives home from *kollel* or work tired and hungry, and of course then the children want to jump on him since they haven't seen him all day, and bedtime has already come and gone, and despite the mother's yelling the children refuse to go to bed, a father might get angry and begin to yell too. Yes, it is very difficult to control oneself in such a situation. Nonetheless, screaming damages.

On a related note: Without good *middos* it is impossible to educate. If a person doesn't work on himself — on his *middos* — he cannot be an educator.

In the book *Minchas Shemuel*, the author quotes his rebbe, Rav Chayim Volozhiner, saying, "Today, harsh language won't be accepted." If we express ourselves harshly, people will not listen to us. People can only hear soft, nice words. "And someone whose nature is not to speak softly, and who angers quickly when people don't do his will, is exempt from the mitzvah of *tochachah* (rebuke)." This is the *psak* (halachic decision) of Rav Chayim Volozhiner: An angry person cannot give *tochachah.*

The mitzvah of chinuch is anchored in the mitzvah of *tochachah.* It seems that an angry person is exempt from chinuch. However, one cannot exempt oneself from chinuch, since ultimately a father remains a father. Therefore, we have no option but to control ourselves. More than 140 years ago Rav Chayim ruled that one should not use harsh language. How much more so today must we avoid harshness, especially with children. Harsh words and actions accomplish nothing. The opposite is true: Harsh words and actions damage. We have no option but to use soft approaches. What should be done when the child doesn't listen? We must express our demand and re-express it until the child listens. This is the wisdom of chinuch: to know how to speak and when to speak.

A related issue is threats. Threats are not healthy. Therefore, it is best to refrain from threatening children. This does not mean that we shouldn't demand things of the child, or that we should give in to him every time he shrugs his shoulders. However, we should not give the child the feeling that he is threatened. We should find a positive way of conveying the demands that need to be made. This is ten times better than the negative approach, the approach that could be classified as threatening.

I cannot emphasize enough the importance of maintaining a pleasant, positive atmosphere in the home. This starts with the relationship between the parents themselves and continues with much thought about creating a peaceful home routine infused with *simchah* (joy).

PROVIDING RESPONSIBILITIES

I would like to mention another essential that could be very helpful in educating children. It is very important to include children in their parents' work. For example: When a new brother is born and returns home, the older brother is often jealous. He feels he has been pushed to the side. Part of the wisdom of chinuch is to include the boy or girl in caring for the newborn, even if the older child is only three years old. It is possible to ask the older child to place the pacifier in his younger brother's mouth, after which the mother should exclaim, "Look, you are my helper!" The older child can be asked to bring something for the newborn or to rock the crib. In this way, the older child will feel he is his mother's partner. This uplifts the child tremendously. With this sort of approach there is no room for jealousy, since the older child identifies with his mother.

The source for this we find in *Parashas Vayetze*. After Lavan chased Ya'akov, the verse records, "And Ya'akov said to his brothers, 'Collect stones.'" (*Bereshis* 31:46). Chazal ask in the midrash (*Bereshis Rabbah* 74:13): Did Ya'akov indeed have brothers? The midrash answers: by "brothers," the Torah means sons. Rashi, in his commentary on the verse, explains these words of Chazal: From the time they were capable of helping him, they were called his brothers. Since they stood by him during a time of need, they became like his partners.

This is a piece of wisdom we learn from Ya'akov — to transform my son into my brother, to convey to the child that in some way he is my equal; he helps me and becomes my partner. He doesn't feel at all that I am burdening him. He does the work with enthusiasm, since the job honors him.

The child who accustoms himself to assisting his parents as a partner gains a new stature. He feels that he has become his parents' brother. This gives children purpose, and through this elevates them and gives them the feeling that they have important stature in the home.

A pathway to stature — the child also receives a position of responsibility, and through this he will grow later into a man who acts responsibly towards those in his home, his family.

CONSISTENCY

Generally, there is no need to make a lot of demands of a child. However, we should not compromise on what we have demanded. If parents see that they must demand something of the child, and they demand it, then they should not back off. They must get the child to accept the demand. Of course, this must be done wisely, in such a way that obviates the need to spank the child or yell at him, but which nevertheless gets the child to accept the demand.

FALSE GOALS

Parents often utilize purportedly educational techniques which, in reality, don't have the slightest connection to their children's education. At the root of these behaviors are selfish, egoistic motivations. Sometimes the parents are driven by completely corrupt traits, traits that the parents would never consider displaying in their relationships with other adults. However, we may exhibit these very traits in our relationships with our children and consider them acceptable: jealousy, hatred, pursuit of honor, anger, conceit, etc., and especially a desire for control. Parents often want to control their children: "The child is under my authority, and I have the right to exercise unconditional power over him."

Here are a few examples of corrupt traits in action.

Jealousy

If I see that the neighbor's child provides his parents with more assistance than my children provide me, I feel jealous: "Why doesn't my child help more!?" If later I force my child to help more, it is possible that I am not being driven by educational theory — by a deep understanding of my child and what is appropriate for him — but by simple jealousy of my neighbor.

Honor

If guests visit, I want my child to greet them nicely and behave pleasantly — not necessarily for the sake of my child's growth, but so that I can elicit compliments from the guests on my superb childraising expertise. Then *I* feel good.

Anger

I feel anger whenever someone violates my will. When it comes to children, there is plenty of opportunity for anger since children often don't behave as we would like.

There are many similarly unpleasant traits that we express in our relationships with children. However, we conceal all these bad traits with the excuse that our behavior is "necessary for educational purposes." If out of anger I strike my child, I might excuse myself saying that it was "educationally necessary." If out of jealousy of a neighbor I make demands of my child, I can fool myself into believing that this too is "educationally necessary." If I want to boost my image in others' eyes through my dear child and, therefore, compel him to act in a particular fashion, this too I can justify as "educationally necessary." In short, exercising total control over my child for entirely selfish motivations can be justified as an educational necessity.

Parents often deceive themselves into thinking that their primary concern is their children's education, when their motivations are really selfish. The net result of this self-deception is that we don't see the child for who he is. We see the child as our property. We think that his purpose on earth is to benefit us, the parents. This is not to say that parents don't feel a responsibility to care for their children. They do. However, too often they do with their children whatever they please. What happened to the principle that we should "Educate a child according to *his way*?" Some parents egocentrically assume that "*his way*" means *their way*. Others recognize that their child has a unique "way" but don't respect it. They think that he should abandon *his way* and adopt *their way* instead.

Another mistake is also common. Often parents place disproportionately high value on those things that they lacked as children. Their intention is certainly good, but their biased perspective can produce disastrous results. Just because a parent lacked something as a child does not mean that his child needs that same thing. Every decision must be carefully and objectively evaluated.

For example, parents who grew up in impoverished circumstances sometimes are adamant that their children will lack nothing. They pour gifts upon their children, often even with lots of concern and love. The children enthusiastically accept the indulgent pampering, but it can ruin their character, God forbid. Overindulgence often produces egoism and selfishness, perfectly fulfilling the verse (*Devarim* 32:15): "Yeshurun became fat and rebelled."

Another example: Sometimes a parent who failed to earn the status he dreamed of in his youth — being a Torah scholar, communal authority, or honored professional — decides to vicariously fulfill himself through his child. He decides, "My child will achieve what I did not!" However, the poor child might have different natural talents that would best be applied in a different field. The child might even have started down his *own* path and might be experiencing real growth and success, and still the parent attempts to crush the child's inborn inclinations. The parent spiritually strangles the child, making clear, "You will be a person of stature, you will learn what I never learned and will reach heights that I never reached!" The child is torn between his nature and his parents' demands. What he is fit to do, his parents won't allow him to pursue. That which his parents force upon him, he has no interest in. The result is failure.

We must know that all these false "educational" goals are not only *not chinuch*; they are the *opposite of chinuch.*

III Central Issues in Chinuch

A DIVINE TRUST

"When I see your skies, the work of your fingers, the moon and stars that you aligned, what is a person that you remember him and man that you entrust him?" (*Tehillim* 8:5)

When David ha-Melech looked at these magnificent creations he was astounded: What is a person that the Holy One remembers him and *entrusts* him? "Entrusts" implies that Hashem gives man a "trust." What is that trust? A child. Hashem expresses His trust in a man by allowing him to become a father, and a man feels this when he becomes a father. The Holy One deposited a trust — a child — in his hands to guard and care for.

There is something distasteful about the statement, "*I have* children." Children don't belong to us. They are not our property. Hashem gave us our children as trusts, and we must guard them.

If a person thinks he has children so that they will care for him when he gets older, or so that he can derive pride from them, he is mistaken. That's not why children are bequeathed to us by Hashem. Children are deposited with us, and we must properly care for this trust, responsibly and reliably.

Earlier we described the two educational processes, planting and building, and we stressed that planting ideally leads to the child's internal potentials sprouting forth. Moshe compared the Torah to rain: "My lesson will drop like rain, my speech will flow like dew, like a downpour upon herbs and like showers upon grass."[6] Once rain saturates the ground, seeds put forth their potential. Once Torah saturates the child, he too puts forth his potential. Of course, we must launch the process by providing all the care to ensure proper growth and development, but the goal must be to produce a self-motivated child who, from deep within himself, yearns to grow in Torah.

Ramban makes this point in his commentary on the first two paragraphs of the Shema.[7] The first paragraph reads, "Teach [Torah concepts] diligently to your children, and *you* should speak of them." The parent or the teacher does the speaking. However, the second paragraph reads, "You should teach [Torah concepts] to your children [so that *your children* will] speak of them."

---

[6] *Devarim* 32:2.

[7] *Devarim* 6:5-9 and 11:13-21.

Indeed, the parent or teacher does the talking in the first stage, but this is not the goal. It is only a transition. In the second stage, described in the second paragraph of the Shema, the children learn to speak on their own. We teach our children *so that* eventually they will learn on their own.

It would be tragic if chinuch smothered this internal desire and initiative.

On one hand, the soul *sprouts*. We must never forget that this is an essential principle: *Include the soul in the educational process*. On the other hand, a mensch is *built*.[8] Such construction consists of developing concrete habits, becoming accustomed to performing mitzvos and living a Jewish life. When we combine these two processes — planting and building, the soul and behavioral habituation — then we are involved in chinuch.

THE OBLIGATION OF PRAYER

The most primary parental obligation is to pray for one's children, and this obligation begins even before the child is born.

We learn this obligation from laws relating to the *Kohen Gadol* (the High Priest): When someone commits manslaughter, the Torah exiles him to a City of Refuge until the *Kohen Gadol* dies.[9] Why is the manslaughterer's term linked to the *Kohen Gadol*'s death? Chazal taught

---

[8] See *Alei Shur*, vol. II, pp. 338-343.

[9] *Vayikra* 35:25-28.

that this constitutes a punishment to the *Kohen Gadol* who should have prayed that no one in his generation kill or be killed. If someone was killed, even if the death happened accidentally, it was a sign that the *Kohen Gadol* failed to pray. Therefore, the manslaughterer's term, which he and those close to him hope and pray will be minimal, is tied to the *Kohen Gadol*'s life span.[10]

Notably, the Torah never explicitly commands the *Kohen Gadol* to pray for his generation. Neither do we find the text of such a prayer included among the special petitions uttered by the *Kohen Gadol* on Yom Kippur. Rather, it is so obvious that the *Kohen Gadol* must pray for his generation that there is no need for an explicit mitzvah or special insertion. Since the *Kohen Gadol* is responsible for his generation, as they are his God-given trust, he must pray for their welfare.

The case of the *Kohen Gadol* is but an illustration of a much larger principle. Anyone who is responsible for others, anyone who has been given a precious trust, is obliged to pray. A rabbi must pray for his community. A teacher must pray for his students. How much more so, a parent must pray for his children. It is clear to me personally that if I have achieved anything in Torah, it is in the merit of my mother's prayers. As a child, I noticed that she prayed for me often, sometimes as much as ten times a day.

We can never pray enough for our children. The obligation is infinite. Our Sages also prescribed no particu-

---

[10] *Makkos* 11a.

lar petition. There exists only the opportunity to pour out our hearts in prayer, and so we must do, each of us composing our own personal entreaty. Our words should address the moment's needs and concerns.

There does exist a general formula composed by the Chazon Ish. Many people include this formula in their Shemoneh Esrei and/or recite it after Shabbos and Yom Tov candlelighting:

> יְהִי רָצוֹן מִלְּפָנֶיךָ ה׳ אֱלוֹקַי וֵאלוֹקֵי אֲבוֹתַי, שֶׁתְּרַחֵם עַל בְּנִי (פְּלוֹנִי) וְתַהֲפֹךְ אֶת לְבָבוֹ לְאַהֲבָה וּלְיִרְאָה אֶת שְׁמֶךָ, לִשְׁקֹד בְּתוֹרָתְךָ הַקְּדוֹשָׁה, וְתָסִיר מִלְּפָנָיו כָּל הַסִּבּוֹת הַמּוֹנְעוֹת אוֹתוֹ מִשְּׁקִידַת תּוֹרָתְךָ הַקְּדוֹשָׁה, וְתָכִין כָּל הַסִּבּוֹת הַמְּבִיאוֹת לְתוֹרָתְךָ הַקְּדוֹשָׁה, כִּי אַתָּה שׁוֹמֵעַ תְּפִלַּת עַמְּךָ יִשְׂרָאֵל בְּרַחֲמִים...

> May it be Your Will, Hashem, my God and God of my forefathers, that You have mercy on my son [name of son], and that You move his heart to love and fear Your Name, and to learn diligently Your holy Torah. May You push away anything that could interfere with his diligent study of Your holy Torah and provide those circumstances that will lead him to study Your holy Torah. For You hear the prayer of Your People, Israel, with compassion...

The concept of praying for our children and their education is so important that one might argue it is the single most important principle of chinuch. It is self-deception to think that the chinuch and growth of our children to be great in Torah and excellent in *middos* is in man's hands, our hands. The matter depends on

Hashem. Indeed, Hashem deposits the children in our hands, and we must fulfill our obligations. But we must pour forth a lot of *tefillah* before Hashem for the deposits with which He has entrusted us.

PERSONAL EXAMPLE: THE FIRST STEP IN PROPERLY CARING FOR OUR TRUSTS

We must realize that even an infant on his first day is already very sensitive to his environment. Every day the child further matures and notices increasingly more detail. We must therefore behave in such a way that we provide an appropriate example.

We find in *Tanna d'Bei Eliyahu* 19:

> "Lift up your hands towards Him for the life of your young children" (*Eichah* 2:19) — From here our Sages learned that a person must beg for mercy on himself, his wife, his children, and the members of his household, that none of them should become involved in sin or inappropriate matters; and that a child should not remain still when he hears his parents speaking unnecessarily; and that if the child does remain still under such circumstances, neither he nor they will live out their days, as the verse says, "Just be careful and diligently guard your soul...."[11]

Here we see the obligation a man has to pray for his family, as we mentioned earlier. However, here we see

---

[11] *Devarim* 4:9.

an additional point: That a son shouldn't remain still when he sees his mother and father speaking needlessly; and if he sees this, he must rebuke them. The child "should not remain still."

And towards the end of this midrash we see how serious the matter is: "If the child does remain still [upon seeing his parents speaking needlessly], neither he nor they will live out their days."

Parents must be careful how they speak. A child can be affected by even once hearing an inappropriate word or dishonorable expression. Also, a child is quite sensitive to his parents' relationship. He listens carefully to yelling. He notices anger. It is impossible to know precisely how spiritually destructive an improper example can be.

Parents must not only avoid anger and other forbidden behaviors, they must also excel in their observance of Halachah. For example, a child will absorb *emunah* from parents who thoughtfully say blessings. This is something even the untrained eye can detect. If, when we say blessings or *Birkas ha-Mazon* (Grace after Meals), we don't mumble, but rather we close our eyes and enunciate the words clearly, even very young children will take notice. What attracts their attention? Infants are accustomed to seeing adults speaking to each other. Mother and father converse, as do parents with their children, and siblings among themselves. The infant notices that one person speaks and the other replies. The infant understands that the noises he hears constitute some sort of communication, an interaction. Then, suddenly, the infant sees a parent speaking with Someone, but that Someone is not visible. The child sees our seriousness, our closed eyes, and our concentration. He knows that we are speaking with Someone important, even though he can't see who that Someone is. At this moment, the child internalizes *emunah*. At a subconscious level the child comes to understand that Someone invisible exists and that we speak with Him. This is a fundamental principle, and the child absorbs it in his infancy… if we say our blessings properly.

We must say *Birkas ha-Mazon* out loud, deliberately and thoughtfully. We must do this for ourselves, and we must do this for our children. Such behavior plants *emunah* in the child long before the child can comprehend sophisticated discourses on issues of faith, and long before the child can even speak.

A child is a constant reminder to parents that they must behave properly, as agents who have been entrusted with a valuable deposit that must be protected.

SEGULOS

We should touch on one other issue related to infancy. The Chazon Ish taught that certain *segulos* have the spiritual ability to help habituate children to *kedushah* (sanctity) and *taharah* (spiritual purity). For example, many people are careful to wash even their infants' hands when the children awaken. Many people are also careful to cover even the youngest boy's head with a *kipah* (skullcap). We should not treat these customs lightly. Even though it sometimes seems that infants don't notice what is happening around them, we know that this is not the case. They are deeply affected by certain actions.

EARLY CHILDHOOD

First words

"When a child knows how to speak, his father should teach him '*Torah tzivah lanu Moshe*,' and if the father fails to do this, he virtually 'buries' the child."[12] The child's first words should be in *Lashon ha-Kodesh* and should be words of Torah. We stressed earlier that one must seize the moment when the child begins to speak, and accustom him to speaking about the Torah and its principles. It should become natural to the child that Torah is the essence of our speech. If we miss the moment, we virtually bury the child since we missed the season for planting an awareness of Torah's holiness.

When a child begins to speak, we also gradually start encouraging him to say *berachos* (blessings). Generally this project is conducted by mothers. One shouldn't get carried away. Mothers should start by teaching their children small prayers that befit the child's level of development. As the child gains fluency, more prayers can be added. Slowly the child can begin saying Modeh Ani, Shema, and slowly, slowly, other blessings too.

---

[12] See above, pp. 19-20.

Mitzvah education

Educating children to do mitzvos also begins at an early age. Performing mitzvos must be a positive experience for a child, and the ideal experience will vary with the child's maturity. Shabbos and singing, tasty treats that accompany mitzvos, and other similarly pleasant associations must be created.

Our Sages also teach that we should draw children into the holidays. Therefore, for example, we give children treats at the Pesach Seder and play dreidel with them on Chanukah.

Shabbos should also be attractive, not oppressive. We should not force children to sit at the Shabbos table for an entire meal. This is too difficult for them, and it is especially hard when guests visit and the meal extends for hours. There are parents who insist on their children's presence at the table *especially* when guests visit, so that they can display how well-trained their children are. This is inadvisable. When it is appropriate for the children to stay at the table, we can attract them with beautiful stories about the weekly *parashah*, or stories about *tzaddikim*, or anything else that creates a fascinating experience and draws them into the event. Children should yearn for Shabbos.

It is also possible to include the children in Shabbos preparations, not in a fashion which makes the child feel burdened, and not just to lighten the parents' responsibilities, but to interest them and give them a feeling that they are "big children," responsible, and partners with their parents.

Like mitzvos and the holidays, Torah study should have positive associations. The Roke'ach describes the wondrous scene on Shavuos when a boy is first introduced to the formal study of Torah. The father takes his child to the synagogue, where the rebbi greets the child and takes him on his lap. The scene resembles the original giving of the Torah, with the rebbi here playing the part of Mount Sinai. The rebbi begins to teach the child the *alef-beis*, smearing honey on each letter and allowing the child to lick it off. A few communities still practice this custom. We must use techniques like this to allow the child, at his level of development, to delight in mitzvos.

CHILDHOOD

Explaining emunah

Slowly, as the child's comprehension develops, we can explain *emunah* to him in language he can understand. A child needs to hear about Hashem. We must tell our child that he was created by Someone, as were we all. We must explain that Someone created the stars, the insects, the flowers, and the grass. It would be tragic if we failed to discuss these important issues with our child.

The child might ask on his own. He might have excellent questions, such as: Where did everything come from? Who made the stars, and Who formed the flowers? Why does fruit grow on trees? Who brings the sun up every morning? When the child asks, the moment has arrived to begin explaining things.

If the child doesn't ask, we read in the Pesach Haggadah, "You must stimulate his question." We must encourage questions from our children and then provide suitable responses.

When children ask where Hashem is, we should explain that He is everywhere. It is not advisable to say that He dwells in the heavens, since today every child is familiar with spaceships, astronauts, and airplanes. If we tell our children that Hashem is in heaven, they could easily misunderstand and become confused. They might conclude that pilots and astronauts meet Hashem "up there in the heavens." Therefore, it is better to explain that Hashem is everywhere, which is true.

We also must be careful not to tell very young children that "Hashem is right here, in this room, with us right now." Very young children can't comprehend Hashem's omnipresence, and the feeling that there is Someone else here Whom they can't see could frighten them. When the child heads off to bed and is alone in his dark room, he will remember that Someone invisible is in the room. This could cause terror or panic. It is better to use the more general explanation, "He is everywhere."

How wondrous are Your deeds!

We must show our children the world's beauty. We probably don't do this enough. One need not travel extensively to see the splendor of Creation. We all have access to fruit. Hothouse or wild flowers are available everywhere. The world's beauty surrounds us if only we open our own and our children's eyes to see it. Of course, if the parents themselves are insensitive to nature's wonders then they cannot hope to inspire their children. It would be sad if a child grew up lacking the emotional development to respond with real awe to Hashem's handiwork. When we contemplate the creation's wonders, we see and absorb *emunah*; and we all need well-developed *emunah*.

Our children's faith will also be strengthened by seeing Hashem's involvement in their daily lives. Rabbi Yechezkel Levinstein *zt"l* once shared with me a technique he used with his daughters. Rabbi Levinstein first explained to them that Hashem runs the world, and then he offered a prize (pocket money) for finding hints of Hashem's involvement in our lives. Through this exercise, Rabbi Levinstein encouraged his daughters to contemplate their environment and notice Hashem's *hashgachah* (Divine providence). I understood from him that he began this sensitization when his daughters were still quite young.

Socializing

Our children start learning how to get along with others around the time they begin preschool. They practice interacting with friends and guests visiting the home, and with acquaintances in the street. Here too, the most important element in the educational process is personal example. The child absorbs the seriousness of the attitude towards welcoming guests and relating to others.

Help and kindness

The child's training in kindness also begins with what he sees at home. It is very important to accustom the child to helping out in the house. Of course, when dealing with small children, their contributions must be modest, and as children mature, so too the assistance they provide at home should grow.

When we are trying to train our children to perform kindness, it doesn't help to force the children against their will. We will not accustom our child to doing kindness with desire and joy through "assignments." We must give our child a good feeling when he helps. We can do this by transforming him into something akin to a "partner" while he is assisting. Then he will feel that he is honored. If a mother includes the child in her work, and a father includes the child in his work, the child feels that he is a partner in the adults' work, and he is honored through this. He achieves a new status in the house, and then he does things out of joy and starts to feel delighted when he helps others.

It is true that in families with many children this process transpires naturally, and the older children assist in caring for the younger children. They become accustomed to assisting and taking responsibility for the little ones. This is wonderful chinuch.

Relating to others and their property

In his first chapter on the laws of theft, Rambam writes, "A *beis din* (Jewish court of law) should punish children in order to discourage [theft] and destructive behaviors." The *Maggid Mishnah* points out that this law has no source in the Talmud or classical commentaries, but is self-evident. *Maggid Mishnah* further notes that this ruling is accepted even by those legal authorities who say the *beis din* has no obligation to prevent children from publicly consuming non-kosher food. Why should a Jewish court treat theft or damage differently from other Torah prohibitions, like eating non-kosher food? Though the court has no responsibility to punish ritual violations by a minor, it is responsible to ensure upright relations between man and his neighbor. Mitzvos that affect our relationships with others have a special status. Therefore Rambam rules that a Jewish court must stop a child from stealing or damaging others' property.

Obviously, parents have more of a responsibility than the court to look after their children's behavior and should pay special attention to their children's relationships with others. We must teach our children not to touch or damage others' property, and to protect what doesn't belong to them. Although these lessons are usually explained in kindergarten in the company of other children, the primary responsibility still falls on the parents' shoulders.

It is also distressingly common that children riding on a bus fail to give up their seats to older passengers. Certainly, this reflects some insufficiency in the schools' curriculum, but such behavior also reveals flaws in the educational program at home. Parents must teach their children to notice others and care about them. It should be obvious to a child that an elderly passenger needs to sit, and the child should enthusiastically and happily offer his place on the bus.

Disagreements between siblings involve unique dynamics and require a unique approach. Here we must allow the children to settle their own disputes, as long as their argument doesn't get out of hand. Such disagreements are natural, and children must get used to settling their own disputes. If a parent does mix into an argument that the children realize they could have settled themselves, usually at least one of the contestants feels he has been treated unfairly. As the Rosh says, "Don't become involved in others' disputes." Although interference might establish temporary peace among the children, it might also stimulate a war between them and the interfering parent.

Questions

Every child eventually begins to ask questions. A child's questions must be treated seriously and addressed directly. If we constantly respond to questions saying things like, "You can't understand this," "You'll understand when you're older," or "Don't ask such silly questions," then we stunt the child's inquisitiveness. The child wants to know, but instead of developing this curiosity, we crush it.

We should celebrate the fact that our child asks questions, and we should answer in a style that matches the child's level of comprehension. When children ask questions that make us uncomfortable or embarrassed, we must still do our best to find and provide serious, satisfying answers.

Shul

We must be careful not to bring our children to *shul* (synagogue) when they are too young. A very young child has no idea what is going on in shul. He is unfamiliar with the prayers, can't read a *siddur* (prayer book), certainly doesn't pray, and he makes it difficult for others present to pray too. We often see such children roaming around the shul during prayers. Very young children naturally frolic and play. They run around the *Aron ha-Kodesh* and *bimah*, and on Rosh Hashanah can sometimes be seen mocking the shofar-blower. It is irresponsible for parents to allow insufficiently mature children into shul.

However, the central problem is not the disturbance in shul. Rather, it is the insensitivity we cultivate when we bring these immature children to shul. A child must appreciate, from the moment his feet cross the threshold, that he is in a special place, a place of *moreh mikdash* — awe of sanctity. We must develop the feeling in our children that it is impossible to play in shul, and we should not bring children who are too young to feel this. The longer we delay the child's first visit to shul, the more the child will understand what transpires there and the better his long-term relationship with shul will be. When a child is brought to shul too early, the shul is transformed into a playground. It will be very difficult to change these patterns of thought and behavior later and to create in an adult the feeling of awe that should have been associated with shul since childhood. Who knows if such damage can ever be repaired.

Sometimes a mother will need some rest, and so the father will take their young child off to shul. The shul thus replaces the day-care center. This certainly cultivates an inappropriate perspective on shul. Of course, arrangements must be made to allow a mother to rest, but shul is not the solution.

If parents must bring a small child to shul, they must watch the child to make certain that he behaves properly. The father should watch his son and make sure that his son's hand never leaves his own hand. One can also bring along a book to synagogue which will hold the child's interest.

Another crucial issue is the choice of shul. It is obviously inappropriate to take a child to a shul where people talk during davening. Prayer must be in a serious place. This seriousness will be absorbed by the child. This is not to say that we should only bring our children to pray in a yeshiva. Prayer in a yeshiva is usually very slow, and it is difficult for children to sit quietly for so long. Rather, we must find a shul that meets these conditions: the prayers should be orderly, there should be no talking during prayers or Torah reading, and the davening should be neither too slow nor too fast.

Ideally, a visit to shul should be a reward. If the child demonstrates that he can behave nicely, then we can grant him a visit to shul. Such an approach increases the prestige of the shul in the child's eyes.

Tefillah clearly requires involving the soul (mentioned above, p.47). If we force a child to act out the external trappings of prayer, or worse, punish him for failing to look as if he is praying, we give prayer a bad taste. When the child grows up, he will have no spiritual connection to prayer, and the sin crouches on the heads[13] of the parents who prematurely forced their child to pray.

SCHOOL

Choosing a school

When we choose a school for our child, we must be careful to select one that values education. Many schools are interested exclusively in packing the children with facts. Often they stuff information into the students and pay no attention to real education; or they ignore the children's conduct, eating habits, or style of play.

Children need to play at recess time, and they can learn tremendous lessons during these breaks. The idea that one shouldn't grab everything for himself but should consider others is generally learned during play. The idea that we don't always win or get what we want can be transmitted during play too. Teachers need to properly guide informal activities. This is the sort of approach we are looking for in our educators and our schools.

---

[13] See *Bereshis* 4:7.

Contests

Today academic contests are popular. During the contest the children learn very well. However, if we track the winners' performance after the competition, we often see that they slack off considerably. Sometimes the honors bequeathed upon the winners blind them and persuade them that they "know it all" already and don't need to continue working. Contests are not all bad, but we need to see the other side of the coin as well.

Desire to learn

Normally, children love to learn. If the parents have a good relationship with their child, and he hasn't been "turned off" to learning, and the parents themselves learn Torah, then the child will want to learn too.

Sometimes, however, a child doesn't want to learn. Such apathy can be caused by a flawed educational environment or burdensome academic load. Rabbenu Yonah writes: "A person must learn to observe children, to understand them, and to discriminate between the perverse and the appropriate."[14] That is, a person must understand his child and comprehend his abilities — what the child can learn now and what he can't. If we see that our child has limited abilities, then we should not send him to a highly pressured academic environment. The child won't keep up, and ultimately the fast pace will break him.

---

[14] *Sha'arei Teshuvah* 3:8.

What should we do when our child doesn't want to learn? The Gemara answers: "In Usha they established that a man should 'roll' with his child until twelve years of age, and then get tough with him."[15] What does it mean to "roll" with one's child? Rashi explains: "If he doesn't want to learn, 'roll' pleasantly with him, with soft words." Persuade him. Entice him. The Talmud recommends that we take this soft approach until age twelve. Of course, today the age has changed, and what was once only appropriate until age twelve is now appropriate until age twenty. Until age twenty we must "roll" with our child.

Boarding schools

Parents sometimes view boarding schools as a social and academic panacea, but living away from home often ends up doing more harm than good. Moreover, the damage can be permanent.

Dormatories have many problems. Among them: A child yearns for his mother's love and the warmth of his home, and he will seek replacements for this affection and comfort. Without proper guidance, the child might find inappropriate replacements. A dorm therefore requires assiduous supervision, and without such diligent surveillance, it can become a nightmare.

Generally, it is better that a child sleep at home. Even if the child wants to stay late at school to study, it is better for him to return home late than to stay over-

---

15 *Kesubos* 50a.

night in the dorm. Slowly this position is gaining ground among parents.

If there is no choice but to enroll a child in a school far from home, it would be best if he could stay with a family there. If this is also impossible and the child must therefore live in the dorm, then the parents must make a special effort to show the child love and stay in touch with him. When the child visits home, the family must celebrate. Love is the one experience that accompanies a person forever. The more love shown to a child, the stronger the child's bond with his parents will be. It is crucial that he see and feel that he is important to them and deeply loved; that his parents worry about him and are interested in his learning and his life; and that his parents call, correspond with, and visit him. All of these efforts are absolutely essential.

On the other hand, one must be careful not to spoil a child. Overindulging a child is as destructive as emotionally starving him. It is well-known that emotionally deprived children and physically pampered children exhibit almost identical symptoms.

THE TEENAGE YEARS

Adolescence

Nothing need be said about the Bar Mitzvah event. Everyone knows how to make a nice party. But adolescence itself, both physical and spiritual, requires analysis.

Parents must forge an intimate relationship with their children and develop such open communication that they can explain to them adolescence and prepare them for the experience. A mother should prepare her daughter, describing what sort of phenomena the girl can expect. If a girl arrives at adolescence without this preparation, she can be so severely traumatized by her first monthly cycle that she might not even recover by the time she gets married.

Boys need preparation too. They need to be taught what a nocturnal emission is so that they are not shocked. This is also an opportunity for a father to explain briefly to his son that sperm is a holy force that will someday make him a father too. At a later age, a little more detail should be added. The Chafetz Chayim spoke with his sons one time when each reached the age of fifteen, and explained to them the details of physical maturity, appropriate conduct, the prohibition on spilling seed, etc. Once in his lifetime, every young boy needs to be presented with all the halachos that apply to this area of his life. Tremendous tests await our youth. What an awesome responsibility parents and teachers have to inoculate the children before they face these challenges!

Finally in this regard, we must do everything in our power to establish separate sleeping quarters for brothers and sisters living at home, especially from age nine and up.

MONEY

A child must become used to relating properly to money. We should give our children a little pocket money. I can't tell you exactly how much to give, but clearly some people give too much.

Children must also be taught not to go into debt. Sometimes I see students buying books right and left. When they run out of cash, they borrow money to continue acquiring books. On the surface, this seems like a positive phenomenon — the child wants to buy books! However, when we ask the child how he intends on paying back the loans, he often doesn't know and answers, "We'll see." Ultimately, the child learns to borrow more money to pay off previous loans, and so the irresponsible cycle continues.

In one of the Chazon Ish's letters he advises *bnei Torah never* to go into debt. We need to cultivate this value in our children. We need to teach them not to go into debt, not to take loans, and not to buy books or anything else when they don't have the money. Even though the merchandise is something truly valuable — like a book — and even though the intention is good, the child must learn not to buy what he can't afford. If the child wants a book, he can ask for a birthday present, but he should never go into debt.

This is critical chinuch for a future Torah scholar! The Gemara[16] records that the verse, "You will gather

[16] *Berachos* 35b.

your grain, oil and wine"[17] (in the second paragraph of the Shema) refers to those who *defy* Hashem's will. The Maharsha asks: How can it be that this verse speaks about someone who *defies* Hashem's will, when it is introduced by the verse, "If you are careful to pay heed to my commandments...," which seems to be talking about someone who *complies* with Hashem's will?

The Maharsha answers: The verse, "You will gather your grain, oil and wine"[18] indeed deals with someone who complies to a degree with Hashem's will, but not entirely. The Maharsha proves this by comparing the first and second paragraphs of the Shema:

In the first paragraph a verse speaks about the obligation to love Hashem with "all your heart, all your soul, and all your might," and our Sages explain that "all your might" means "all your money."[19] A nearly identical verse appears in the second paragraph, but there the words "with all your might" — with all your money — are absent. That is, the second paragraph speaks about someone who fails to serve Hashem with all his money. His heart and soul serve Hashem, but not his money. In financial matters he is not so religious.

The punishment is measure for measure: He struggles to earn a living — "*You will gather* your grain, oil and wine." The person described in the first paragraph of Shema, who serves Hashem with all his money too, is

---

[17] *Devarim* 11:14.

[18] Ibid.

[19] *Berachos* 54a.

rewarded measure for measure: "Teach your children diligently, and speak [of Torah concepts] when you sit in your house and when you travel on the way..." This man is freed of financial pressures so that he can concentrate on his Torah studies.

The primary preparation to make Torah our profession, to serve Hashem "with all your might" — with all your money — is to avoid debt except under the most extraordinary circumstances (like saving a life). We must teach our children that before they spend they must evaluate whether Hashem approves of this expenditure. The first step in making this assessment is to ask: "Do I have money to pay for this?" The child must accustom himself to thinking: "If I have money, then I may buy; but if I don't have money, then I shouldn't buy."

Of course, if the children see the parents living beyond their means, purchasing even when they don't have money to pay and going into debt, we cannot expect the children to behave differently.

Going into debt is spiritually suicidal. When a budding scholar makes purchases beyond his means, he finds himself taking out one loan to pay off another. He spends his time and energy juggling finances, and the first casualty is the immersion in Torah. Financial concerns devour his attention, destroying his Torah studies and prayer. If we want our child to achieve a true connection to Torah, we must accustom him early on to spend only those funds that he possesses and never to go into debt.

These are painful matters to discuss, and they affect marriage plans too. A young couple that is compelled to enter into debt in order to live in the city would be better off if they would go to a small town where housing is less expensive, where they wouldn't need to go into debt, and where the husband could learn more peacefully. Some object that in small towns the *kollel* is less good: "It's not like Yerushalayim or Bnei Brak!" True, but the husband will learn better in a small town than in Yerushalayim or Bnei Brak, since his head will be free to learn, while in the big cities he would be distracted by financial concerns.

YOUNG ADULTHOOD

Rebuke

Earlier we referred to the Talmudic discussion about when a child is no longer fit for rebuke: at age sixteen or twenty-four.[20] The Meiri strikes an interesting compromise, explaining that the ideal age for rebuke is *between* sixteen and twenty-four years old.

Rebuke consists of clarification.[21] We must clarify to a child, and especially to a young adult, what constitutes good behavior, what his personal characteristics are, etc. The Meiri writes that ages sixteen to twenty-four are ideal for this sort of clarification. Of course, rebuke is necessary even before age sixteen. But the ideal window

---

[20] *Kiddushin* 30a.

[21] See *Alei Shur* vol. I, p.278.

of opportunity — a period when one can speak openly and deeply about personal issues — is this eight-year slot.

SHIDDUCHIM

It is impossible to establish a particular age when children should start looking for a spouse. Sometimes parents feel their child is ready to get married long before the child is interested. In such cases, parents should not push their child to begin the process.

The opposite is also true: If a nineteen-year-old boy approaches his parents interested in looking for a wife, parents should not necessarily discourage him just because of his age; young people often know what they need. If our children say that they need to get married, we must take the request seriously.

Additionally, when our children do begin dating, we must not pressure in any way. Getting married is the most personal decision our children will ever make. Only they can decide with whom they should go out, or how long they should date. Unfathomable pain has been caused by parents and others who pressure children to get married. For example, I once spoke with a young man who had gotten engaged two months earlier. When I met him, the man complained that he had no desire whatsoever to marry his fiancée. I asked him, “If so, why did you get engaged? Why did you select this girl?” He answered, “My grandmother’s step-aunt said this was the right girl, and the parents too, and the aunt also...” Oh, what pain they caused! They told him that everything would be okay, and that wasn't true. If we force our children into such a marriage, we can imagine what their home will look like.

If a couple dates for a period, and one of them feels that there is no common language, or no chemistry, under no circumstances should we advise the couple to get engaged. Our child is unsure? Let him or her think! Only the child can decide. Our child should think for as long as he or she wants. If the child ultimately feels unsure, he or she shouldn't marry. It is forbidden for anyone to pressure a child into marriage.

Conclusion

The Midrash records[22]:

> Eliyahu says: When someone increases Hashem's honor and decreases his own honor, both Hashem's and his own honor increase. When someone reduces Hashem's honor and increases his own honor, Hashem's honor is unaffected but his own honor decreases.
>
> Once there was a man praying in shul alongside his young son [during the festival of Sukkos]. While all the people answered "*Hallelukah*," the boy called out silly things. The people told the father, "Look at your son saying silly things." The father responded, "What should I do with him? He is a child. Let him play!" The next day the same thing happened. All the people were singing "Amen, *hallelukah*," but the boy called out silly things. The people told the father, "Look at your son saying silly things." The father responded, "What should I do with him? He is a child. Let him play!" All eight days of the holiday the boy called out silly things, and the father never said a word to him. Far before their time the father and his wife died, as did the boy and the boy's own son.

---

22 *Bemidbar Rabbah* 4.

This is a portrait of someone who ignores his educational obligations. The father said, "He is a child. Let him play!" But the father was wrong, since parents have a responsibility to increase Hashem's honor by raising children with *Yiras Shamayim* (fear of Heaven).

Education is a huge responsibility. A person's whole mission in this world is to guard the trust the Holy One gave us — to raise this child/"trust" with all our strength and to appreciate the responsibility we parents have to set a good example.

We must learn how to give our child a *Torahdik* soul, not just mechanical habits or technical knowledge about how to behave. By "soul" we mean the joy, beauty and splendor of fulfilling a mitzvah; we mean the taste of a mitzvah. We must show our children their purpose and mission in this world. We must open their eyes to the wonders of creation too. When we plant *emunah* like this in a child, there is hope that the child will grow into someone who independently yearns to study Torah and perform mitzvos. When he himself wants to grow, then we have hit the educational target.

Education is compared to lighting the menorah in the *Beis ha-Mikdash*. "When you lift up the flames," the verse says[23]; and Rashi comments: The pilot torch must be held in place until the flames rise independently from the menorah's lamp. A parent must ignite the soul of his child until the flames of love for Torah rise on their own.

---

[23] *Vayikra* 8:1.

Glossary

The following glossary provides a partial explanation of some of the Hebrew and Yiddish words and phrases used in this book. The spelling and explanations reflect the way a specific word is used herein.

ARON HAKODESH: the Holy Ark that holds the Torah scrolls in the synagogue.

BEINONI: a person of average character.

BEIS DIN: a Jewish court of law.

BEIS HA-MIKDASH: the Holy Temple in Jerusalem.

BIMAH: the platform in the synagogue from which the Torah is read and from where the prayers are led.

BIRKAS HA-MAZON: the Grace after Meals.

BNEI TORAH: people whose first priority in life is Torah study.

CHASSIDUS: piety.

CHAZAL: a Hebrew acronym for "our Sages of blessed memory."

CHINUCH: education.

DAVID HA-MELECH: King David.

EMUNAH: belief.

ERETZ YISRAEL: the Land of Israel.

GEULAH: redemption.

HALACHAH (pl. HALACHOS): Jewish law(s).

HASHEM: God.

HASHGACHAH: Divine providence.

KEDUSHAH: sanctity.

KIPAH: a skullcap.

KOACH HA-TZEMICHAH: innate growth potential.

KOHEN GADOL: the High Priest.

KOLLEL: institute for advanced Talmudic study.

LASHON HA-KODESH: the Holy Tongue, i.e. Hebrew.

LIFNEI IVER: "Do not place a stumbling block before the blind" (*Vayikra* 19:14); i.e., do not misguide the uninformed.

MA'ALOS: good qualities.

MASHGIACH: spiritual supervisor.

MASHIACH: the Messiah.

MAZAL: the astrological sign which determines a person's character.

MECHANECH: educator.

MENSCH: (Y.) an emotionally mature, spiritually refined human being.

MIDDOS: character traits.

MILAH: circumcision.

MITZVAH (pl. MITZVOS): commandment(s).

MOHEL: ritual circumciser.

MOREH MIKDASH: awe of sanctity.

MOSHE RABBENU: (the prophet) Moses our teacher.

PSAK: halachic decision.

RASHA: a wicked person.

ROSH CHODESH: the first day of the Jewish month.

ROSH YESHIVAH: the dean of a yeshiva.

SEGULOS (sing. SEGULAH): supra-logical actions that have practical effects.

SHEMONEH ESREI: the Eighteen Benedictions or Amidah prayer.

SHIDDUCH: a marital match.

SHOCHET: a ritual slaughterer.

SHUL: (Y.) a synagogue.

SIDDUR: the prayer book.

SIMCHAH: joy.

TAHARAH: spiritual purity.

TALMID CHACHAM: a Torah scholar.

TANACH: an acronym for *Torah*, *Nevi'im* (Prophets), *CH(K)etuvim* (Writings); i.e. the Bible.

TEFILLAH: prayer.

TOCHACHAH: rebuke.

TORAHDIK: (Y.) infused with Torah.

TZADDIK: a righteous person.

TZEMACH: a plant.

YESHIVAH KETANAH: a yeshiva secondary school.

YIRAS SHAMAYIM: fear of Heaven.

ZT"L: a Hebrew acronym for "may the memory of the righteous be for a blessing."